LOVE MOSTLY, AND OTHER LIFE THINGS

Taé

BookLeaf Publishing
India | USA | UK

Presentation by BookLeaf Publishing

Web: www.bookleafpub.com

E-mail: info@bookleafpub.com

ISBN : 9789358361254

First edition 2021

To my mother for always supporting me

with my creative pursuits and

encouraging me to be myself

PREFACE

This book is a dream come true - a long overdue goal that seemed attainable through the help of Instagram, time being right, and conveniently a lockdown.

I remember back to my first stumbles at writing, I used to read stories out of a blank notebook my mother gave me. One of my very first poems is still hanging in my mums kitchen; a cut out fish with a poem about it on the back.

I have gifted countless poems to old flames, dear friends and people I thought needed words to comfort them.

Now I hope that you dear reader, can join my thoughts for a while and enjoy my words too.

1

Your heart is but a song

With a melody which is not soft as snow

Nor loud as a brash man's cuss

But strong as a vast seas breeze

It brushed past like a stealthy cat

And surprised me like the eyes of an owl

I did not expect such felicitation

Or such honesty and naive persuasion

My heart paced

I knew not what to do

Or whether what I assumed

Was what you meant too

I reread what you wrote

I tried to cool my emotions

Surely, it's just a myriad

Of jumbled conversations

Hints but uncertainty

Like a newly learned dance

Which has not yet been perfected

For performance

I stumbled

I withdrew

Without

Really wanting to

My politeness

Is like a double-edged sword

It saves me but slays me

When I least want it to

Talking in riddles

Walking in circles

I found myself smiling

And falling asleep thankful

That if somehow life were almost

perfectly right

And if the chance was slight

We just might

Be alright

2

A fool would move so fast

Impatient with quips of desire

Quite surprised

That this folly should transpire

Learn'ed thoughts and actions doth

disappear To places which should

instead remain near

Oh, how I chide myself

For my frippery

My words do cast away

Any feeling that would from you come

my way

Oh childish heart

That so moved

Should run at speed

And fall upon itself

How I beat myself

Like my heartbeat too

When I thought any such thing

Should be between us two

Oh folly heart

Oh banished soul

Let this be a lesson

To us all

3

I don't know which way is up
I keep searching and always find myself
at the bottom again

Everything I know is turning around me
And the more I move
The more I keep falling to where
I don't want to be
I can't stay still for very long
And I'm always looking for that
helping hand
That one who will stop me from
falling
But I always think I've found them
before I land
I hope one day this to and fro will stop

And I won't feel so dizzy

From this constant uncertainty

4

Talking to be polite

But both knowing there's something else

there

Hidden, not showing itself

Like a shadow

It creeps closer

And halts our conversation.

A wry smile

A brush of the hand

And my body melts into yours

Like sea into hot sand

Our lips meet and part

And your confidence grows

Your eyes flicker like flame in a storm

And soon you stop apologising for your

desire

Hands traverse skin covered by
decency
Lips invite decency to be exposed
Revealing shades of curiosity
Now unveiled and known
Lying together
Is like being underwater
Submerged in a giant lake
The weight is heavy, yet effortless
Trying to find the surface
Yet wanting to stay in this moment
Our bodies fight for air
Yet in this fury,
we succumb
to its fatality
Our last breath, we take together
Like the final stroke
Or the final chord
Of a masterpiece

5

If sin is this beautiful

Does it make it right?

Why am I so comfortable with this?

When I know what to do

Maybe for once

I am sick of playing by the rules

Time and time again

My purpose has been revealed

Healing, and making sense of the

hidden truth

So, for some reason

I feel like there's a reason to this

imperfect situation

And if my place to come is hell

I know it well

6

If I only get to love you for a year

It will still be love.

If you are using me

Let me use you too.

If that's how you can settle it within

yourself

Console yourself with this mutual truth.

I might only be some temporary fix

But you will have my undivided attention

I will be yours for as long as you'll have

me

Desire has always been a fine line

between delirium and dysphoria

Let me always hunger for you

Until we let go of each other.

Waiting for you to text

Is like waiting to be able to breathe

You just hope you won't die.

And then you forget about dying

Because hearing from you

is more important than remembering

not to expire.

You are like the air in my lungs

The words in my mouth

When I hear from you

The clock restarts.

Holding your hand, being with you

Was feeling like a kid in a candy store

But your charm is just

some good luck

you would throw away

to anyone

Engaged to M.L.

Whoever she is she is one lucky girl

Soon to be one of 10…

How stupid could I be!

Swept up in your sweet smile

Your chocolate brown eyes

And your need to pleasure and be

pleasured.

Getting in your last fix

Before tying the knot, prepared to take

her and some others over the threshold

of desire.

Being prepared; is that what you call it?

I won't sully her name again;

I'll tread carefully before you have your

way with me

You text me

In the early hours

Broken from sleep or broken from life

I will hold my judgement

It is not for me to rush to this conclusion

Who am I to make such judgement?

That is reserved for only one, who has

given to me life

I will ask, and hold my accusations

And seek forgiveness for my actions on

behalf of us

Life has brought you forward into my

world

Let me be grateful for the lessons that

you hold

I will continue to learn the secrets you

will reveal.

And I hope that between us we will heal.

7

I held my heart out to you

And you filled it with what it

wanted to feel

But behind those actions was an

emptiness

That was greater than what you gave

At first, love was the feeling of seeing

you smile

The sound of your voice

The touch of your hand

The many moments we spent together

But time holds no value in these things

When I started to think about all the

times

I did things for you and held you up

above myself

I soon grew to realise that you had

learnt to look down on me

You thought you had surpassed me

And so, you left me behind

All I want

Is to realise as closely as possible

a love which extends itself

and is correct in the eyes of God

Through it,

I hope better to understand myself

and the one

whom I love

8

Love is more than my giving

More than your sweet lips and soft smile

Love is satisfied

It is enough

It does not search for something else

It is selfless, not selfish

It does not tread casually

It does not tempt

You have something

A precious gift

A woman who was there when no one

else was

And yet you want more.

I have nothing

Except my heart

And a willingness to be chosen

by a heart that is pure

And does not seek the carnage of lust
and lies
Please ask yourself the tough questions
About why she does not hold the
greatest value
The reason why you cannot see
anything but her in your world
Do not charm me with your loose words
I once fell for it
But this time, I must choose the right
path

9

I'm sorry I am so quiet

When we are together

I always want to be there for you

To listen and to care

And then I forget,

I, myself am there

So please let me tell you

Somethings you should know

about me too

For such a colourful person

I can be quite shy

My decisions are made

where my heart lies

I have known many people

but I still feel alone

I am quite deep and so it's hard to find

someone willing to listen and learn

To follow me, my dreams and to find in

someone, a home

I've grown to realise I'm not just

summed up by what I do

And that faith is something that is

integral to the actions I choose

For a long time, I have always accepted

relationships where I can help others

But you can imagine with a profession

like teaching and giving in relationships

I end up feeling used

I am most afraid that I will never find

the love I am searching for

And that if I am too choosy

In this life my endless searching

will be my ruse

I have almost always known who I am

And I don't apologise for that

But I will always apologise

When I am not in the right

10

I've always tried to do the right thing

Forgoing situations which are not right

But for some reason

I'm stuck on you

My heart is drawn to the feeling I get

from your sensitivity

The openness, your willingness to listen

It means a lot that you are on my side

I've never felt the pure joy I get from

your goofy faces, your sweet smile, your

cinnamon eyes

Even when you are eager to please

I love how much you are willing to give

And I'd never take advantage of that

When you first held my hand, I wanted
to cry because
I'd forgotten that feeling of wanting to
skip down the street
I'd forgotten that feeling of being
someone's 'someone'
I'd abandoned it on the side-line
between my to-do list, feeding my cat,
staying home
And being content that I wasn't tied
down with a baby and a mortgage

I'm a mixture of Benjamin Button and
Peter Pan
Never really wanting to grow up
and then realising when I wake up from
this dream that life goals have passed
me by

I'm always on the edge of

if the right person came along

held out their hand

and told me to jump

We would be each other's forever

But despite this

I trust that life has a plan for me

and that if I keep my heart open

The right path will present itself.

11

Sometimes

I hear us making love

In a progression of chords

In guitars

Effects pedals

And synth pads

When I hear it

You are never there

You always slink off home

I wish you could stay

Wake up and realise you don't love her

anymore

But I am dreaming the impossible

12

When this ends

I can no longer look into your eyes

I can no longer feel your warmth

We can no longer pretend we are happy

I can no longer hold your hand

I will forget to be carefree

Like a butterfly

Our feelings will fade into

not meant to be

My heart took a risk

I gambled on an impure stake

I never knew how happy I could be

With someone as unhappy as me

You thought I would oblige

And for a while I did

And then your wifey came to me

Saying she knew exactly what you did

You assumed she would not notice

A different look a different feel

You acted so invincible

Like it wasn't a big deal

Now your silence and separation

Gives me some kind of sense

That all those plan b scenarios

Were just a bit of gas

And maybe now you're reeling

From the choice you chose to make

Your 'brain' made a decision

Which then begot your fate

The past

is a door I leave closed

But the past

It doesn't politely knock

It invites itself in

Gets comfortable

I'm not exactly welcoming but I'm not

rude My subtleties, too subtle

The past

Keeps telling me about how great it is

I'm not listening

I've learnt my lesson

But it's still there

And I haven't exactly asked it to leave

But I hope

It eventually gets the message.

14

I understand it now

The evening joint

The cool

The magic as the smoke

dances with the air

The dark

A guilty pleasure

A slender smile

As everything unnecessary disappears

I'm a dreamer

But this sweet smoke

Filled within it a whimsy

A story

Which hangs delicately around me

As if I'm watching the universe

My head inside a snow globe

The stars dance

like the artificial snow

15

Shadow

Without you, there is no presence of light

So, whilst you lurk

I shine bright

You are my soft place to fall

I do not fear you, no not at all

I hope to find a friend for you

Someone who will walk beside you,

To keep you close, to keep you warm

And for two parts

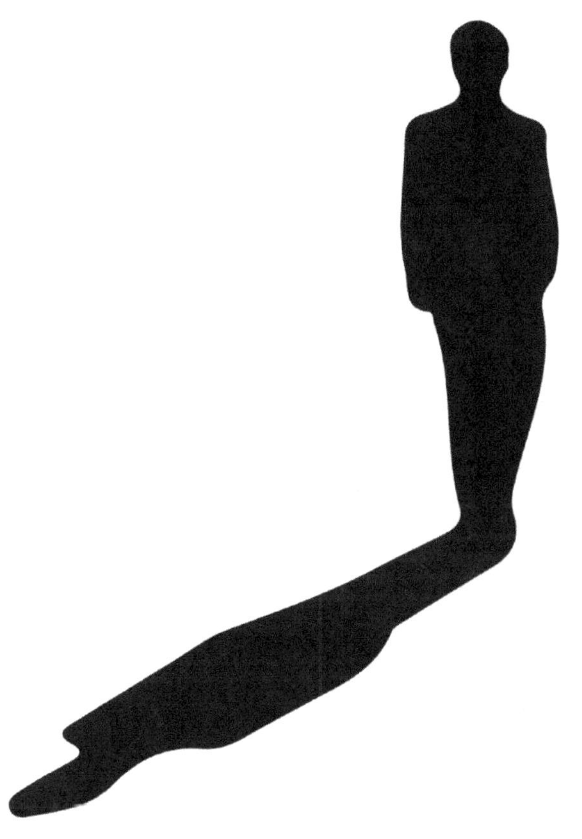

16

My mind

Free of all its troubles

Whilst my eyes were closed

Gave me wings to fly

What I gained was

A perspective that I often don't have the

privilege of experiencing too often

confined by the paths and roads that my

feet are forced to take

A freedom from myself

A vessel of burden, responsibility

hanging upon it like ornaments

My body, lightened like the air which

carries me

It's the only time you are trying to control

the duration of something so beautiful

whilst being totally out of control in your

subconscious.

Why is it, when we are awake

We forget this simplicity?

If only I could close off my eyes,

Turn off my mind,

Open my arms

And fly

I feel beautiful

When you look at me

With that look, that I am the only thing

you want to see

When you sneak in like I wasn't

expecting you at all

And the way you hold me

Just that little bit longer than normal

That feeling

I know you feel it too

I try not to fall so fast

When you ask me not to

You say you don't know the future

But the present is more than I can ask

for

Just one and the other

That is what's perfect

You try to annoy me

But I like you too much for it to affect me

That's not a challenge though

If that's what you expect

I remember our first kiss

How unexpected was all of this?!

The more and more your fingers and

mine want to link

The closer we get

lying together, breathing in sync

Our heart beats in time and I start to

think

If this is now

What future bliss is to come?

What you and I will become?

18

Dream

That is what I thought this was

I could not imagine I deserved this gift

You came

When I needed you most

I prayed for you

And dreamt of who you would be

And there you came

19

I'm not sure why the hostility

So many lives lost

And all we want to do

is protect as many as we can

So we have to stay at home

Netflix and playing on the phone

Sleep-ins and day long snuggles

A chance to connect and actually focus

on ourself and one another.

For others the silence and loneliness

aches

Like a solitary prison that no one can

break

A single cell with the floodlight on

Can make or break a particular person

Then there are the super shakers

Making hay while the seeds barely sown

Online business working from home

Finding hope where hopelessness
groans

So, we now at Lockdown 4.0

Anxiety, frustration, and a menagerie of

personal feelings flow But safe at home

is where I'll be

Doing my bit for society.

20

For a while there I was dormant

Just within myself

Waiting for the right moment to

Burst forth and take what's mine

I lost my confidence,

My passion, my drive

Just investing my knowledge into small

humans that just ask 'Why?'

Every day, the same routine

Get up, work, no in-between

No, What is something that I can do?

An investment for my future too

Hope can only come to those who look

Seeking to find some knowledge, a

crook

A ladder to a place unknown

Until the learning becomes known

I'm glad I stepped outside my shell

The dear old place had become hell

Day by day my eyes 'come wide

With learning that can be my guide.

You can't have runny eggs

When you're living on the go

Runny eggs are the types of things

You can only eat while slow

Order them at brunch

Or at home with a pot of tea

Runny egg life

Is the kind of life for me

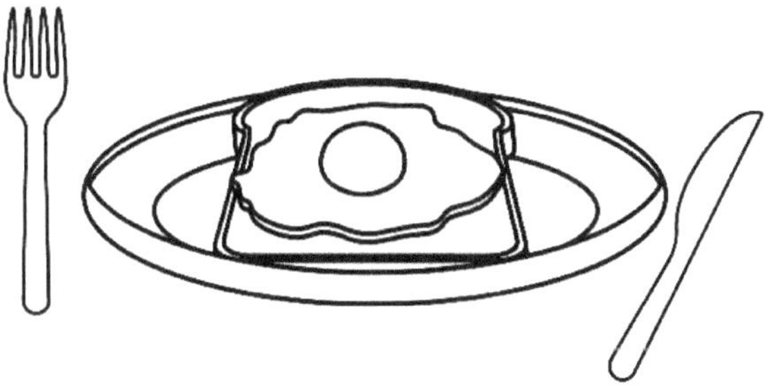

22

The older I get

The more I realise

That most people

Can't live a life without lies

Any excuse

Is something they'll do

To get out of something

They'd rather not do

What happened to pushing

The limits of what

Your own expectations

Had thought was your lot

Maybe each time

Is a chance for you

To grow a little

And live truthfully too

23

Cat cuddles

They aren't the same as normal ones

They are smaller, softer

and sometimes scratchier

Like a dandelion's seeds

Your fur gets caught in the air

and scatters

Falling about anywhere

I'm not sure how many times

You need to adjust yourself

Just to find

The same position

But cat cuddles

Are something that

I know

I can't live without

24

I try to imagine myself as a

businesswoman

Sat at a desk in my skirt and shirt

High heels, semi kicked off under the

desk

Hair in immaculate fashion, probably

brown

At 35, I couldn't be further from this

Living my 'Peter Pan' life

Blue hair atm, tattoo's, make my own

clothes

Teaching music, playing in shows

I wonder if I could ever be

That business type, 'professional' me

The one that possibly, my mum could

see

Before I started to explore my
individuality
I wonder if at last I should grow up
Be the version that people pin up
The model vision of society
The one that we aspire to be
But I digress, I have never been
The type to take things easily
The left
of center,
wild child
BTW I've always kept the wildness mild
So just before my 36
I reflect on what should come next

So, here's to another year from this
crazy fool
Never let your dreams be someone
else's version of you

25

A quick one

To end it all

Thanks so much

Hope you've had a ball

'Twas pleasure

That I found in words

When I was just

A little girl

Then onto Shakespeare

Then to Poe

And even some

Maya Angelou

Plath and Wordsworth

Yeats and Keats

I loved them words

like some love beats

I hope dear reader

Yes, that's you

That mere words continue to mean

something to you

And so dear reader I say adieu

I hope you might share these words

With someone

You know will like them too.

www.ingramcontent.com/pod-product-compliance
Lightning Source LLC
LaVergne TN
LVHW050938200726
843508LV00011B/2370